YOGA: THE EARLY STORY

Seeking the Source

by

Gill Lloyd

RB

Rossendale Books

Published by Lulu Enterprises Inc.
3101 Hillsborough Street
Suite 210
Raleigh, NC 27607-5436
United States of America

Published in paperback 2015
Category: Philosophy

ISBN : 978-1-326-23449-2

Dedication

This book is dedicated to my teacher TKV Desikachar with thanks for the teachings he has shared and for all the years he has tirelessly given of his knowledge and wisdom.

Acknowledgements

I started this task many years ago whilst on a post-graduate course with Paul Harvey so I want to thank him for setting me off on this journey of discovery.

I also want to thank Karen Adamson, Sarah Ryan and Ray Lloyd for their proof-reading of the drafts and their helpful suggestions.

Many thanks too go to Simon Low for so kindly writing the foreword and for his on-going encouragement and support.

Finally, this would not have come to fruition without the help of Mandy Beaumont who has generously given many hours to preparing this for publication.

To all, my deepest thanks.
Gill Lloyd

CONTENTS

Foreword by Simon Low 7

Preface 10

Introduction 13

The Veda-s 16

The Principal Upaniṣad-s 18

- Taittirīya Upaniṣad (T.Up.) 20
- Kaṭha Upaniṣad (K.Up.) 24
- Śvetāśvatara Upaniṣad (Śv.Up.) 27
- Maitri Upaniṣad (M.Up.) 30

Vedic Teaching - Śruti 34

The Bhagavad Gītā (BG) 35

The Yoga Sūtra (YS) 38

Summary 43

The Significance of Oṁ 45

Selected Verses for Further Reflection 48

Author's Background in Yoga 52

Bibliography 56

Foreword by Simon Low

Gill Lloyd is a truly authentic reflection of yoga's teachings, a cherished friend and a faculty colleague at The Yoga Academy. I have had the pleasure of knowing her personally for nearly 20 years, and with each year I more profoundly experience the depth and breadth of her knowledge, and her great skill and generosity in its sharing. This book is an encapsulation of Gill's study of yoga's historical progression through textual reference, offering yoga teachers and interested students of yoga a clear and supported journey through time and teachings.

Unlike many yoga authors, Gill is offering all the tools for you to cultivate your own perspective and to personalise your experience without attempting to entice you to any one way of thinking or learning. Gill has done the arduous work for you of scouring the primary texts associated with yoga's development over the millennia, and presents the information in a manner that can benefit all, whatever your chosen approach or style of yoga, or even your understanding of what yoga has been, is, or can be to the individual. The textual inclusions are clearly referenced, pictures have been added to offer appropriate visual accompaniment and enjoyment, and there is a very helpful section on 'Oṁ', a sound, word and intention much used within the yoga world, often with insufficient understanding or respect. Gill's attention to this often sketched over subject will be of value to all readers.

Within and between Gill's words we hear the voice, feel the heart and can benefit from the teachings of her teacher, mentor and friend, TKV Desikachar, considered by many to be one of the most important teachers of modern times. In fact, it was at a lecture day by TKV Desikachar at the Bharata Vidya Bhavan centre in London, where I first met and was so warmly welcomed into the yoga community by Gill.

The authenticating of yoga's teachings by way of sourcing the teachings from ancient or more contemporary texts is an on-going tradition. This seems clear by the many occasions where ancient texts have been used to give weight and licence to approaches to and styles of yoga, and equally to much of their content.

Within this offering Gill skilfully invites the reader to use textual reference as a ground to help shape, support and validate their own personal understanding, and to see how the ancient allusions can help us avoid illusion, even delusion.

Sourced historical documentation is of immense interest to many, and offers valuable landmarks. Gill Lloyd does a sterling job for us all by bringing these landmarks into a simple and accessible format, offering us ample space for our own conclusions, and excellent foundations for our on-going enquiry.

Enjoy and enrich your studies.

Simon Low

Founder and Principal of The Yoga Academy

Preface

This work started life as part of my thesis for Viniyoga Britain - it evolved into a useful booklet for students on the Yoga Academy Teacher Training course and I have since been asked to make it more widely available - hence this publication.

The purpose of this work is to offer a practical guide for anyone interested in the origins of yoga, especially for those who find themselves overwhelmed by the sheer volume of literature to go through and the differing styles of presentation and archaic language. I have tried to flag up where yoga emerged as a distinct path and to follow its evolution. The seeking out of that path is not simple because the stepping stones are often far apart.

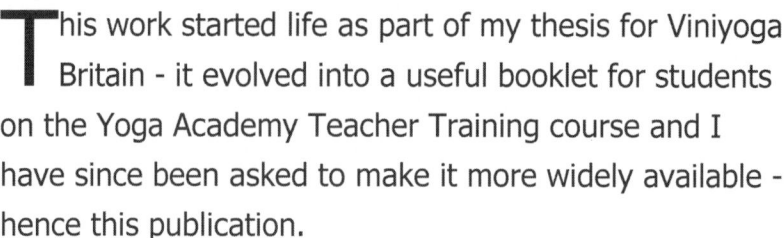

Rather than employ a more narrative style, I have to some extent sacrificed more imaginative prose and chosen to build the piece from the original texts. I have used my interpretations to keep the language simple and the message clear. I have highlighted the passages where the word yoga actually appears (at times this is like seeking diamonds in a coal mine – the odd glimmer here and there). I do realise that this can at times make the reading a little dry but my overarching objective has been to offer something that is above all practical and helpful for yoga teachers and students.

Yoga teachers often get asked the questions "where did yoga start", "how old is it", "what was its original purpose", etc. This book should make the answering of these questions easier. I have done the detective work in extracting the key references and tried to present these in a readily accessible format for those who want it. It may also provide a stimulus for further study for those so minded.

What I have offered here is a very simplified overview. I hope I have included and encompassed all the major landmarks of Yoga's history that may inspire further reading and study for other yoga practitioners. I have given more space to the Upaniṣad-s perhaps. This is because they are such large texts and the references to yoga harder to find in their somewhat archaic prose. I thought the extrapolation might prove helpful.

N.B. I have not included later Tantric literature and emergence of haṭha yoga from about 800CE onwards.

These develop the topics of āsana, cakra etc - for example in the Haṭha Yoga Pradīpikā (HYP).

Introduction

The Yoga Sūtra of Patañjali is regarded as the pivotal yoga text. It is the basis for all yoga studies and practice. The eight limbs of yoga (aṣṭaṅga) as presented by Patañjali are known by most of the many millions that count themselves as yoga practitioners today. The text itself is studied in detail by serious yoga practitioners and is the main resource for yoga teachers.

It was probably composed in India around 200-300 CE, at a time when there was a great upsurge in philosophical thought and debate about the nature of existence and reality. Its culmination was the six schools of Indian philosophy, the Sat Darśana-s: Yoga, Sāmkhya, Vedānta, Mīmānsā, Nyāya and Vaiśeśika.

Of these six, the classical yoga perspective is provided by the Yoga Sūtra of Patañjali. In this, he offers a journey towards a clear understanding of, and insight into, our true nature and purpose, providing many avenues to explore and tools to employ to make the attempt successful. We are offered glimpses of the light at the journey's end, the elusive understanding of who and what we are and the obstacles that we may encounter along the way.

Did this work emerge from Patañjali's contemplation alone (no doubt at least shared with his students), or did it have roots in earlier traditions and history? To answer this, we need to look briefly at what preceded even the Upaniṣad-s. Patañjali's work comes as the pinnacle of a mountain of earlier thought, introspection and observation and it has drawn together the basic strands to define the very essence of yoga. So, what went before? What are the seeds and where is the soil in which these great teachings emerged?

We must go as far back in Indian history as we can, right back to 1,500 BCE and beyond, when a society flourished along the banks of the Indus Valley. The archaeological sites of Mohenjo Daro and Harrappa (now in Pakistan) have revealed the way of life of an affluent trading people set in sophisticated town planning and architecture. Amongst the archaeological finds at these sites were numerous seals, some of which depict a man seated in a meditation pose, giving an intimation that these people already had an experience of Yogic teachings and practices. These seals, though quite small, are of incredible beauty (one can be seen in the National Museum of Delhi). So we know that trade and business were not these people's only interest: there are clear signs of a spiritual tradition. From this ancient culture and people came the oldest scriptures known to man – the Veda-s.

The Veda-s

These four works are considered to be the four pillars of ancient Indian thought on which subsequent teachings rest for authority and authenticity. Of the four Veda-s, the most famous and the oldest is the Ṛg Veda, followed by the Sāma Veda, the Yajur Veda and the Atharva Veda.

They are attributed to illumined sages who are said to have heard these mystical teachings directly from God. Their language is both poetic and symbolic and directs the aspirant on the path to spiritual enlightenment.

These four Veda-s do not describe yoga in a technical sense. This honour belongs to the Upaniṣads. But what they do is hint at yogic thought. For instance, in the Ṛg Veda appears a poem called "The Hymn to the Long Haired One". In this we are given a vision of an ascetic who has great powers (siddhi) and certainly intimations of the archetypal Yogi: one free from the fetters that bind the common man. The Ṛg Veda also includes the Gāyatrī Mantra. Although of Vedic rather than Yogic origin, it has made its way across the centuries into the consciousness of many a yoga practitioner today and can be found woven into their daily practice, e.g. as silent repetition in prānāyāma and meditation. There are also the concepts of agni and sūrya, seeds for techniques like agni sara and sūrya namaskāra.

Their teachings about life and spiritual purpose were developed further in texts known as Brāhmana-s and Āranyaka-s. The culmination of all these earlier texts is provided in the Principal Upaniṣad-s and is referred to as Vedānta, i.e. the end of the Vedas. They were composed over a period from around 800 to 300 BCE.

It can thus be seen that traces of yoga are present in these most ancient of works, but it is not until the Upaniṣad-s that yoga emerges as a distinct concept and it is here that it develops, opens and flowers.

The Principal Upaniṣad-s

The word Upaniṣad indicates sitting close to a master to receive secret and sacred teachings, and the texts themselves are regarded as the essence and culmination of the Vedic hymnodies. Particular families (lineages) took an on-going responsibility for particular Veda-s and their related Upaniṣad-s. Composed over many centuries by various sages thought to have come from both the Brahmin and Kṣatriya varna-s or castes, they are poetic discourses on the human condition and offer the possibility of freedom and liberation from all that oppresses mankind and the transcendence of the normal limitations of the human condition.

Of the early principal Upaniṣad-s (Bṛhad-Āraṇyaka, Chāndogya, Taittirīya, Kauṣītakī, Aitareya, Kena, Kaṭha, Iśa, Śvetāśvatara, Muṇḍaka, Praśna, Maitrī and Māṇḍūkya, it is interesting to note that the actual epithet YOGA is found in only four: Taittirīya, Kaṭha, Śvetāśvatara and Maitrī, and that these four all come from the lineage of the Black Yajur Veda (the Yajur Veda has two branches: the Black and the White, following a split of the lineage). It appears that it is this particular grouping which has been the arena for Yoga's conception and evolution. We must now explore these texts for what they tell us about what yoga meant for these people – and to pick up where the ideas are forerunners for yoga concepts developed in the Bhagavad Gītā and the later Yoga Sūtra.

Taittirīya Upaniṣad (T.Up.)
circa 700 BCE

One of the earliest Upaniṣad-s, its style is not easily accessible. It consists of 3 chapters or Vallī-s.

The first Vallī includes many statements on the roles and well-being of teacher and student and correct procedures in all aspects of life are emphasised. It also gives the rules for chanting, an essential discipline for ensuring the correct transmission of these texts, so vital for an oral tradition.

It is in the second Vallī that we find yoga mentioned for the very first time. This Vallī describes a person as having five aspects: anna maya – the body made of food, which is filled with prāṇa maya, the aspect of breath and energy; mano maya, our mental faculties and the learning we have received; vijñāna maya, our personality and value system, and ānanda maya, the seat of our emotions and happiness. Each maya is described as a bird with a head, tail, right and left wings and a body. It is in the description of the vijñāna maya that yoga is found, representing the body of the bird. Its head is said to be śraddhā, (faith, trust), the right wing ṛtam (absolute truth), the left wing satyam (how we express the truth) and the tail mahat (the great beyond from which we have emerged). Commentators on this work all suggest that the word yoga here refers to contemplation and the idea of the quiet mind.

This model of the human system is still very much part of yoga teaching today and comes in to its own when working with individuals and in therapy situations. The need to assess where a student's problems come from, i.e. whether they are physical, psychological or emotional, and choose suitable techniques to help them towards health and well-being.

In this model we are introduced to yoga and also to its accompanying concepts of faith, righteousness and truth. These too are seen as fundamental to later yoga practice and link with the yama and niyama of Patañjali's eightfold path.

The five aspects presented in the second Vallī are explored again in the third, as a journey of meditative enquiry. Here we find the concept of yogakśema, the idea of being able to stay with our practice and not lose what we have gained.

Great emphasis is made in the T.Up. of knowledge as the liberating expedient. We shall see this take a major role in the later Bhagavad Gītā under the banner of Jñana Yoga, the yoga of wisdom and understanding. The other factor highlighted here is the role of teaching. Prayers are offered that the teacher may find good students, that the teaching may be effective and that the teacher and the student together be protected in the enterprise: "May he protect us both. May he be pleased with us both. May we work together with vigour. May our study be illumined. May there be no dispute between us. AUM. Peace, peace, peace." T.Up. Chap 2, v1:

sa ha nā vavatu
sa ha nau bhunaktu
sa ha vīryaṃ karavāvahai
tejas vinā vadhitamastu
mā vidviṣā vahai
Oṁ śāntiḥ śāntiḥ śāntiḥ

This prayer is as relevant now as ever, expressing the crucial importance of preserving a sound transmission within a safe and supportive environment and is in common usage among many yoga practitioners today.

Although yoga as a clearly developed discipline is not presented in this text, certainly aspects of yoga which are developed later, are mentioned here.

Kaṭha Upaniṣad (K.Up.)
circa 500-400 BCE

Here references to yoga become more explicit and numerous. Apart from the term yoga itself, the text also endorses the need for a competent teacher, the idea of reverence, the use of mantra and the need for non-attachment, knowledge and understanding. In many ways, it is more accessible than the T.Up. and we are offered ideas supported by a rationale, and a clearer description of the path to take.

The style is in story form. It is about the encounter of a young Brahmin boy, Naciketas, with Yama, the god of death. Yama offers the boy three boons. His third and key request is to know what happens after death. Does anything still exist? Yama is most reluctant to deal with this but he gradually reveals more to his persistent questioner.

Within this dialogue yoga is afforded a more prominent and delineated role. For the first time in history, we are given an explanation as to what this term actually refers to and means.

"When the senses and the mind both stop their usual functioning and the intellect is steady, this is said to be the highest state.
This state is called yoga, where the senses etc are controlled." **Ch2, Sect3, vs10&11**

In **Ch1, Sect3, v3**, this control of the senses is expressed in an analogy. The senses are likened to horses pulling a chariot (the body) which must be kept under control by the charioteer (the intellect/buddhi) in order that the passenger (the true self/ātma) can reach his true destination. This clearly links to Patañjali's eightfold path, where sense control and the withdrawal of the senses from external stimuli are natural concomitants of the meditative journey. Patañjali's own definition of yoga, in YS Ch1 v2, is the ability to direct the mind towards an object without interruption or distraction, and to stay with it. This implies that the mind should not be swayed by the senses. The Bhagavad Gītā also discusses this. Krishna talks of the wisdom of one whose senses are restrained and the firmness of that wisdom (BG Ch2 v68). Thus we see the basic tenet of the YS is rooted in much earlier teachings.

Similarly, in **Ch1, Sect2 v12** of the K.Up. we find the concept of Adhyatma-yoga, the process of self-realisation through meditation.

Other aspects of yoga are also found in the K.Up. and great emphasis is placed on the roles of knowledge and understanding. We find these ideas picked up by Patañjali in both Kriyā and Aṣṭaṅga Yoga as Svādhyāya, which is both study and self-observation. In the final verse of the **K.Up. Sect6 v18**, the term yoga is used again: Nachiketas, having received knowledge given by Yama and the entire rules of yoga, was free from passion and free from death and so may any other who understands this about the soul. Again mastery of the senses and the path of knowledge are aligned with yoga. This final statement endorses yoga and emphasises the high regard in which it was held by this time.

Śvetāśvatara Upaniṣad (Śv.Up.) circa 500-400 BCE

So far, we have been introduced to yoga and given a definition. Now we are offered some practical advice on how to proceed. This is dealt with in **Ch2 v8-15,** which will be discussed verse by verse. In these eight verses, we are taken through the complete yoga journey, from finding the right environment, to what posture we should adopt and how we should breathe. We learn of manifestations that may occur, the physical attributes that are gained and of the ultimate release from all that binds us.

v8 Provides the first instruction, which is to assume the correct seated posture with spine erect, both for meditation and control of the breath. This is a fundamental teaching in all schools of yoga whether from the Rāja or Haṭha perspective and advocated in both the Bhagavad Gītā and the Haṭha Yoga Pradīpikā. The second issue is the withdrawal of the senses as part of the transcendental process echoing the teachings both of the K.Up. and the YS.

v9 Tells us for the first time that the restraint of the breath has a role to play and reminds us that the thought waves of the mind have to be restrained and directed appropriately. As in the K.Up. the chariot analogy is invoked to emphasise these ideas.

v10 Explains the need to be in the right environment to practise, one that is clean and agreeable and private. Although life today is so different from these ancient times our basic need for a place conducive to yogic practice is the same. We need enough space, a clean floor and an agreeable temperature, all away from unhelpful disturbances.

v11 We are introduced here to the phenomena that may occur during meditation. We find echoes of these in YS Ch3 with the attainment of special powers (Siddhi) that manifest as a consequence of samyama (dhāraṇā, dhyāna and samādhi) and again in the final chapter of the HYP.

v12 Explains that for the adept, sickness, old age and death no longer have any influence on him. Absolutely nothing disturbs him.

v13 Links first signs of progress in yoga with lightness, healthiness, a clear complexion, a pleasant voice, a sweet smell and scant excretions. We have similar claims in the YS and the HYP. We are told in very clear terms of the practical benefits of yoga practice, resonating strongly with modern concerns.

v14 Tells us that when the self has fulfilled its purpose and is free from sorrow it is like a dusty mirror that has been cleaned and now is clear.

v15 Here a second analogy is used to denote the goal being reached: that of the soul as a lamp shining brightly. Then we are told "we are free from all fetters". This phrase occurs so frequently in the Upaniṣads that it could almost have the status of a "Mahā Vākya" a great saying expressing the core of the teachings.

We are thus given the full spectrum of yoga. Later texts and schools certainly elaborate on and develop these concepts but all adhere to this basic framework.

Maitri Upaniṣad (M.Up.)
circa 300 BCE

This is the last Upaniṣad of the Black Yajur Veda lineage and is twice the length of its predecessors. It commences with a discourse between Bṛhadratha, a king who had renounced his kingdom and was practising extreme austerities in the forest, and Śākāyanya, the knower of the Self. The dialogue is somewhat similar to that between Naciketas and Yama, Śākāyanya prevaricating but eventually revealing his answer by telling stories within stories. Yoga is given wide coverage in this text and many scholars consider it instrumental in its development. I have again dealt with this by reference to the text.

Ch4 v4 offers a three pronged approach of knowledge, austerity and meditation. This is very much akin to Patañjali's path of Kriyā Yoga which consists of discipline (tapas) self-study (Svādhyāya) and the acknowledgement of a higher principle or force (īśvara-praṇidhāna).

Ch6 v18 describes six limbs of yoga which are practices to effect unity. These consist of prānāyāma (breath control), pratyāhāra (sense-withdrawal), dhyāna (meditation) dhāranā (concentration) tarka (contemplation) and samādhi (complete absorption in the object of meditation). Although not dealing with lifestyle, personal observances and āsana, as Patañjali does in his eight limbs of yoga, its main aim is the same. The journey goes in the same direction.

Ch6 v20 acknowledges different levels of accomplishment and suggests progression in levels of meditation, just as Patañjali offers different levels of practice, detachment and samadhi.

Ch6 v21 Here we find the use of the breath and the reciting of the syllable AUM, both linking with practices in the YS. Also there is a clear forerunner of later Haṭha techniques with the concept of the suṣumnā, the prime energy channel of the subtle body; jihvā bandha, the tongue lock, and the use of breath and sound. They are common to both Rāja and Haṭha teachings.

Ch6 v22 links back to earlier teachings in this lineage, of the soul dwelling in the heart. It also offers the concept of Nāda (inner sound) and the closing of the ears to experience it. These ideas are fulsomely developed in the much later Haṭha Yoga Pradīpikā (HYP).

Ch6 v25 draws this all together into a definition of yoga: yoga is said to be when the breath, mind and senses are at one and when we have let go of all the demands of existence.

Ch6 v27 poetically expresses the heights of yoga: the space in the heart is where we find the highest and yoga too.

Ch6 v28 tells us how we can be successful on our yoga path and warns of the dangers of over-attachment. As propounded by Patañjali, vairāgya (non-attachment) is seen as essential for the ultimate realms of yoga to be attained.

Ch6 v29 concludes this section on yoga with the following: through the practice of yoga one becomes content and experiences tranquility and is no longer disturbed by the perils of opposites. The rationale for taking the yoga path is once again eloquently expressed and once more, one cannot fail to see the links with Patañjali's teaching. Saṃtoṣa (contentment) is one of the 'niyama', the second aspect of the eightfold path. He also talks about the vanquishing of the pairs of opposites through the practice of 'āsana', its third aspect.

Finally, we are enjoined not to give this teaching away too lightly. It continues to clarify that these teachings are very special and should not be given away carelessly. They should only be offered appropriately, to those able to work with them with respect and understanding. This is clear guidance for teachers that the teachings must be passed on appropriately and with respect.

Vedic Teaching - Śruti

All the four Veda, the Brahmanā-s, the Āranyaka and the Principal Upaniṣad-s, are referred to as the Vedic Canon and are given the epithet ŚRUTI, which means "that which was heard". These great compositions are regarded as the very words of God, heard by ancient sages in deep meditation. As a collection, they are regarded as the most sacred texts of India's religious history.

Around the time of these later Upaniṣad-s came another religious text that has yoga as a continuous theme. One of the most famous texts in religious history, the Bhagavad Gītā is the second most-translated book in the world after the Bible. It comes under a group of works referred to as SMṚTI, which means "that which is remembered". Although this deems the BG to be of lesser status than the Veda-s, in popular esteem it is ranked amongst them.

The Bhagavad Gītā (BG)

The Bhagavad Gītā is a section of the great Indian epic, the Mahābhārata. The BG takes the form of a dialogue between Arjuna, a warrior on the side of righteousness, and Lord Krishna who is his charioteer. Just as the fighting is about to begin, Arjuna is struck down by doubt as to the worthiness of this engagement and is overcome by despair. Krishna leads Arjuna from a point of abject misery through a voyage of discovery, gradually revealing the purpose of life itself. It is done step by step as Arjuna's attitude changes and he opens to new ideas. Krishna is here the wise yoga master, teaching as is appropriate to his student, leading him skilfully towards the goals of clarity and insight, the very goals of the Upaniṣad-s and the later Yoga Sūtra.

The BG, although written in an age so different from our own, has a distinct resonance with the dilemmas of today. Arjuna is in the midst of disputes among his family, friends and teachers – a problem not confined to ancient history! It certainly has much to offer both as a guide to understanding and as a comfort, as we try to follow the yoga path.

Although the main focus is the concept of dharma (doing one's duty and living righteously), yogic references abound and, indeed, each chapter is called a 'Yoga'. Various well known paths are explained including 'Karma Yoga' (the yoga of action), 'Jñana Yoga' (the yoga of wisdom) and 'Bhakti Yoga' (the yoga of devotion). 'Dhyāna Yoga', the title of Ch6 (the yoga of meditation), offers a practical approach with ideas about where to practise, how to sit, how to breathe and where to focus one's attention. It also gives the rewards for whoever has such a disciplined mind. This very much echoes the practice of yoga as portrayed in the Śv. Up., detailed earlier.

The BG also gives a number of definitions of yoga:

"yoga is evenness of mind" **Ch2 v48 & Ch6 v33**

"yoga is skill in action" **Ch2 v50**

"yoga is the renunciation of selfish purpose" **Ch6 v2**

"yoga is a harmony in all that we do" **Ch6 v16**

"yoga is the unlinking of the link with pain" **Ch6 v23**

Each of these can be appropriate at different times and in different situations in daily life for Yogis, past and present, and together they show the depth of yoga and its adaptability.

The BG teaches us about the fundamental nature of matter as represented by the three guna-s, the three basic qualities of inertia, activity and clarity, which make up everything in the world of matter. These are said to have a profound influence on all our behaviour. This subject is pursued in great detail, with guidance on how to transcend the pull they have on us. The teachings of abhyāsa (practice) and vairāgya (dispassion) in Ch6 give the clearest yoga teaching on how to transcend the sway of the guna-s, through disciplining both mind and body. Abhyāsa represents the positive things that should be present in our lives. Vairāgya is identifying those things that are unhelpful and unsupportive of our yoga journey, loosening our attachment to them and leaving them behind.

These two ideas are also the first practical teachings offered by Patañjali (YS Ch1 v12). That they occur in both such major works on yoga only serves to endorse their importance and significance.

Finally, the BG offers support and comfort, especially when things go wrong. For example, Krishna offers the comforting words that any of our efforts on the path of yoga will protect us and progress will be made! (BG Ch2 v40).

The Yoga Sūtra (YS)

So we return to where we started: The Yoga Sūtra, a secular text that has become the central pre-eminent teaching on yoga, not superseded in the respect given to it since its compilation. Other texts have followed but all refer to the YS as being at the heart of yogic thinking. It is studied and chanted and followed as a life guide by sincere followers of yoga across the globe. The fact that it does not insist on any one belief system and is free from cultural leanings has been the key to its universal acceptance. What a prescient man Patañjali must have been! However, apart from his undoubted brilliance and wisdom, we actually know very little about him and his life. The stories that do exist have a mystical and mythical quality. For example, he is often referred to as Ādiśeṣā, the serpent upon whom the god Vishnu rests. Statues and paintings often depict him

as a man emerging from a coiled snake, its hood providing a canopy for him.

Patañjali composed his treatise in Sūtra form, aphorisms or short pithy statements requiring a teacher to expound them to reveal their full meaning. It is here that we find many of the ideas first hinted at in the Veda-s, drawn more clearly in the Upaniṣad-s and the BG, now being brought together in one single text solely focused on yoga. It is a brief work of 195 Sūtra. Its four pāda (chapters) are overviewed here to identify a few of the more important links:

Ch1 introduces yoga and its meaning and purpose. It tells of the obstacles we may encounter on the path and gives various suggestions for overcoming them. It concludes with the ultimate state of yoga, Nirbīja Samādhi (meditation without seed, i.e. not linked to anything, neither concept nor object.)

Ch2 introduces Kriyā Yoga (the yoga of action): tapas (disciplined practice), Svādhyāya (study) and Īśvara-praṇidhāna (devotion to the highest principle). The purpose of Kriyā Yoga is to give a feeling for meditation and to overcome the kleśa (fundamental issues we all have as human beings). It goes on to deal with the symptoms and causes of our sufferings and shows the way forward to the goal of freedom from all this. It is here that aṣṭaṅga (aṣṭa meaning eight, aṅga meaning limbs or components) yoga is listed as the eightfold path leading to prajña (insight) and viveka (discrimination). The first five limbs are described: yama (social conduct), niyama (personal restraint), āsana (posture), prānāyāma (breath control) and pratyahāra (turning the senses away from external stimuli).

Ch3 completes the eight-limb model with dhāranā (concentration), dhyāna (meditation) and samādhi (absorption). The process of these three is called samyama and Patañjali then gives many examples for meditative practice, but also offers warnings against being side-tracked by powers gained along the way.

Ch4 tells us that although powers can be gained in various ways, the only reliable path is through the aṣṭaṅga path to Samādhi. It is someone who has taken this route that is the most reliable teacher. Patañjali then picks up earlier themes and concludes with the term Kaivalya, a concept of the utter freedom of a completely clear mind.

This text is the culmination of the meditative enquiries of sages over thousands of years, expressed so clearly that it leads students of today along the path, offering guidance, purpose and understanding. It has not been superseded for 2000 years. It truly speaks for men of all times and I am sure will continue as a beacon into the far distant future.

Summary

These ancient teachings have been preserved for us, over thousands of years, with love and devotion. We should remember that this has all been made possible by the skills our forebears had in oral transmission. So if we find the reading of these texts somewhat dry and dusty, we can explore chanting them as the ancients did themselves and gain a feeling for the sounds as well as the intellectual understanding of these works. This can reveal hidden depths and beauty, suggesting more than words alone can express, so that we may avail ourselves of their wisdom, which despite the passage of time, has real significance for the modern world.

Indeed yoga continues to evolve and serve the communities in which it emerges. Yoga today has enormous popularity - in the UK nearly every village has a weekly yoga class. These classes undoubtedly feature āsana and relaxation as the main components, but this often leads to questioning and a desire to know more. Hopefully, this work may be of service here.

Reviewing this enquiry, we find that our first encounter with yoga was in the Taittirīya School. From that time, yoga has come to mean something very special, wonderfully encapsulating all that we consider to be within its orbit. It may well be that this inspired choice of epithet - yoga – has indeed yoked all these diverse works and teachings together, thus ensuring yoga's role for the people of today and of tomorrow. Although today our world is externally unrecognisable from the times discussed here, our underlying human condition has not changed. We are still vulnerable to the undertow of anger, greed, desire, etc., and we are still searching for elusive happiness and contentment. These ancient sages discovered the understanding of these problems and their solutions and we can find solace and direction through their teachings today. We should give thanks to these early teachers for all they gave us so long ago and to all those who have brought the teachings down the centuries through their selfless commitment and devotion.

The Significance of Oṁ

As with yoga itself Oṁ is a sacred gift from India. It is so ancient that it cannot be dated. For Hindus, Buddhists and Jains it represents the infinite divine - the absolute that dwells in our hearts. It is placed before sacred texts and mantras to denote that the words come from a divine source which were given voice to by the ancient Seers/Ṛṣi. It is often used this way today in yoga settings as invocations such as the prayer for wellbeing, strength and harmony between teacher and student e.g. Oṁ śāntiḥ śāntiḥ śāntiḥ

In the Māṇḍūkhya Upaniṣad which is solely on Oṁ - it tells us that it consists of 'A' 'U' and 'M' ('A' + 'U' in Sanskrit becomes 'O'), the letters symbolising waking, dreaming and dreamless sleep. In the Yoga Sūtras of Patañjali - he refers to Oṁ as the praṇava - PRA = special, NAVA = new/boat i.e. that which takes us across all the obstacles that come our way in life. He tells us that we will come to understand its meaning through its recitation. The concept of sound being the origin of life and the universe is common to many traditions e.g. in St

John's Gospel "In the beginning was the word, and the word was with God, and the word was God".

In yoga, whose roots are in these ancient Upaniṣad-s, we have taken it to refer to the very essence (ātmā) of ourselves and the essence of the universe thus linking these two together (yoga means to link). However, we should use it wisely, carefully, with respect and awe. We should not abuse the gift bestowed to us.

Controversially, many years back, my teacher TKV Desikachar, requested his teachers to stop using oṁ in general classes because he did not want us to offend anyone or to stop them practising yoga because of cultural or religious misunderstandings. He caused quite a stir in Zinal, Switzerland at a big yoga convention saying that the yoga world was using oṁ too casually. Arguments ensued but it did stop everyone in their tracks and make them reflect on these issues. In his centre in Chennai there are no religious symbols at all - only a picture of his father Professor T.Krishnamacharya and a statue of Patañjali in the garden. He wanted people of all religions to be welcome.

This may seem a heavy caution but history has deemed this necessary. We should reflect that the svastika is an ancient symbol of the sun, decorating temples all over India and is also a yoga āsana - svastikāsana. But because some in the West have distorted both its form and meaning, it has become a symbol of darkness rather than of light in our Western culture.

So when we want to share oṁ with others, we should think first and teach as it applies to those we are teaching, rather than ourselves. We can use it freely ourselves and with all who are happy to embrace this gift.

Selected Verses for Further Reflection

I have chosen a few verses that I hope will inspire you to pick up the texts and read them in a fuller context. Along the way you will almost certainly find new treasures and insights to support you on your own personal journey.

ON WISDOM

K.Up Ch1 Section2 vs1+2

We are offered two different paths to follow in life. One is for the good, the other follows pleasure. The wise man should consider this and discriminate, choosing the good rather than the pleasant. The unwise choose the pleasant only for worldly reasons.

ON IGNORANCE

K.Up Ch1 Sect2 v5

Many a fool thinks himself wise and leads others but this is like the blind leading the blind.

ON STAYING ON THE PATH OF YOGA

K.Up Ch1 Sect3 v14

Wise men declare that the path we tread is as sharp as a razor's edge and difficult to follow (this quote was the source for the title of Somerset Maugham's book 'The Razor's Edge').

ON PRĀNĀYĀMA

B.G. Ch4 v29

For some they focus on prānāyāma, the path chosen towards selflessness.

B.G. Ch5 v27

The focus on the breath in the nostrils and controlling its length is here part of the meditation process.

ON COURAGE

B.G. Ch4 v42

Arise, Arjuna, having used the sword of wisdom to cut away the doubts that you felt in your heart (a product of your ignorance).

ON NON-ATTACHMENT

B.G. Ch5 v12

One who practices yoga with discipline and is not concerned about the fruits of his actions, will experience a peaceful state of being. The undisciplined, concerned about rewards is bound by feelings of desire.

ON FREEDOM

B.G. Ch5 v28

The wise man whose aim is freedom, whose senses, mind and intellect are controlled; who has become free of desire, anger and fear, is forever free.

ON WHERE TO PRACTICE

B.G. Ch6 v11

For practice, one should find a suitable place to sit, in a clean place, at the right elevation, covered by a cloth, an antelope skin and kusha grass (although the practical details are for a different age, the message is the same. We need a clean, quiet place to practice, free from distractions - again, the distractions may be different but the principle remains the same).

ON 'THE GOAL'

B.G. Ch6 v19

His soul (i.e. the yogi) is like a candle flame when it is undisturbed by any breeze (a poetic vision of the yogic state of harmony & oneness).

ON 'YOGA IN DAILY LIFE'

B.G. Ch6 v9

One who remains even amongst friends or foes and can remain neutral, is to be respected amongst men.

YS Ch1 v33

Friendliness to all; compassion for all in need; gladness for all that have achieved good things; and seeking understanding in dark situations will lead us to a state of tranquility.

Author's Background in Yoga

For over 40 years Gill has been a dedicated practitioner of yoga and from early days in her yoga journey has followed the teaching of TKV Desikachar (full details below). Gill was introduced to this teaching whilst on a British Wheel of Yoga (BWY) teacher training course in 1976 and recalls being struck by the rationality and intelligence of its approach. During the ensuing years, she pursued her studies directly with TKV Desikachar and other teachers practising in this lineage.

Many years ago Gill met Indira Devi, then aged 92 (the first western woman ever to be taught yoga by Prof. T. Krishnamacharya, TKV Desikachar's father). She asked Gill who her teacher was and upon hearing that she followed the teaching of Sri TKV Desikachar, Indira responded "Wonderful! He is the greatest teacher to come out of India today. Excellent!" Gill feels that the years since have only served to prove this true and she expresses enormous gratitude to have received TKV Desikachar's guidance.

TKV Desikachar

Born in Mysore in 1938 in to a noted yoga lineage, his father was the great yoga master: **Professor T. Krishnamacharya**. He had a formal education culminating with a degree in engineering. Shortly after starting his career in this field, he took a complete volte-face and determined to become a yoga teacher after a realisation of the great skills and knowledge his father was offering. He asked his father to be his teacher and guide; staying at his side and learning from him until his death on 28th February 1989, aged 100. Desikachar founded the Krishnamacharya Yoga Mandiram in Chennai (KYM) in his father's honour.

Early on in TKV Desikachar's yoga teaching and studies, his father asked him to teach the great philosopher, J. Krishnamurti under his guidance. This led to TKV Desikachar accompanying Krishnamurti on a lecture tour in Europe and began his involvement with western students, many of whom consequently committed themselves to 2-3 years of study with him in India. As they in turn returned home, they set out to spread the tradition to a wider western audience with the main message that yoga practice needs to be tailored to suit the individual - like bespoke tailoring rather than "off the peg."

TKV Desikachar's impact on yoga across the globe has been huge and his best selling book "The Heart of Yoga" is on the bookshelf of almost every yoga teacher and serious student. It presents all the tools of yoga and shows that yoga is far greater than āsana (posture work) alone. He shows how prānāyāma (controlled breath work) meditation, chanting and study all have a part to play on the road to well-being. He has a great gift for presenting ancient teachings in a meaningful way that inspire and inform yoga practice.

His life and work have been dedicated to guiding and helping others on their path: a true inspiration to all yogis.

Written by Gill Lloyd, 2014

In 1977 Gill gained her BWY Diploma and went on to teach groups of students locally - in 1982 she was appointed as a Diploma Course Tutor to train new yoga teachers. In 1987, whilst running her third BWY Teacher Training Course, Gill enrolled on a four-year course with Paul Harvey to focus on the tradition of Prof. Krishnamacharya & TKV Desikachar - and followed that with a post-graduate course. Throughout these further trainings, Gill focussed on the yogic application (to the reality of life in today's world) of āsana, prānāyāma, meditation, chanting and the study of Vedic literature. Yoga in the tradition of Prof Krishnamacharya & TKV Desikachar plays great emphasis on the need for practice to be tailored to the individual and adapted for different stages of life and personal circumstances, so this tradition focusses on 1-1 teaching. Gill supplemented these studies with frequent study trips to the KYM where she then became a direct student of TKV Desikachar himself.

In the mid '90s Gill was voted as the first director of Viniyoga Britain (later to become AYS). Gill was asked by TKV Desikachar, when he set up an Indian centric training in 2006, to be one of its founding trainers for 'KHYF UK' which later became 'TSYP'.

Today Gill teaches mostly in the UK but has also taught in Southern Ireland, Austria, France, Pakistan, Israel and India. She currently runs study groups for teachers, leads a Vedic Chant sanga, teaches individuals and speaks at yoga seminars. Since 2005 Gill has been Tutor of the 'Philosophy Module' on The Yoga Academy's Teacher Training courses in the UK.

Gill has, for many years, regularly taken interested groups out to India - both to study at the KYM in Chennai and to explore sacred sites of Southern India.

Gill is clear in her efforts to offer yoga as a holistic approach to meet contemporary needs, whilst still being based on authentic yoga teachings. As Gill says "although the world has changed dramatically, basic human nature and its essential needs have not. Yoga is a treasure trove of wise advice on the human condition that supports our quest for contentment and well-being." Gill seeks, both through her teaching and in this book "to share these gifts to all who may be interested."

written by Mandy Beaumont
(taken from a 2014 interview with the author)

Bibliography

The Principal Upaniṣads
Translator: S. Radhakrishnan
Publisher: Indus/Harper-Collins I.

The Bhagavad Gītā
Translator: Winthrop Sargeant
Publisher: State University of New York Press

Reflections on the Yoga Sūtras of Patañjali
Translation and Commentary: TKV Desikachar
Publisher: Krishnamacharya Yoga Mandiram

The Bhagavad Gītā
Translator: Juan Mascaro
Publisher: Penguin